# JESUS
### *of*
# NAZARETH

# FRANCES LINCOLN
in association with
## National Gallery of Art, Washington

# INTRODUCTION

Jesus grew up in Nazareth, a small city in the countryside. He was neither rich nor powerful, but in spite of this, the story of his life has influenced countless people throughout the world, and has been told again and again, in words and in images, for nearly two thousand years.

The Gospels do not tell us what Jesus looked like, so artists used their own imaginations when they painted scenes from his life. The pictures in this book were painted at a time when few people could read, so that the events had to be shown to them in pictures. To make the stories come alive, the artists put in details that were familiar from daily life, so that the clothes, the buildings and the backgrounds in each painting tell us about the artist's own world. The main focus is always on Jesus himself, but his face and the setting are different each time, depending on when and where the artist lived.

These pictures were painted between the fourteenth and the seventeenth centuries, when many rich patrons paid for works of art to hang in splendid churches. They were seen as a gift to God, and as an aid to prayer for the people who came to worship. They are painted with great skill and care, and use glowing, expensive colours – gold, red and blue.

The words come from the Authorized Version of the Bible, a seventeenth-century translation of the Scriptures into English. People have used this version since the time of Shakespeare and the Pilgrim Fathers, and the language in which the story is told has helped to shape the way we all think of Jesus.

As you turn the pages of this book, words and paintings take you from the annunciation of Jesus' birth and his nativity, through his boyhood and events from his ministry, to his crucifixion and ascension into heaven. All the episodes are part of the same story, but each picture is very different, a triumph of individual skill and imagination.

JOY RICHARDSON

# The NATIVITY

And it came to pass in those days, that there went out a decree from Caesar Augustus, that all the world should be taxed. And all went to be taxed, every one into his own city. And Joseph also went up from Galilee, out of the city of Nazareth, into Judaea, unto the city of David, which is called Bethlehem; to be taxed with Mary his espoused wife, being great with child.

And so it was, that, while they were there, the days were accomplished that she should be delivered. And she brought forth her firstborn son, and wrapped him in swaddling clothes, and laid him in a manger; because there was no room for them in the inn.

LUKE 2

# The FLIGHT into EGYPT

*Three wise men told King Herod that Jesus was the King of the Jews. Herod ordered his soldiers to find and kill the baby.*

And, behold, the angel of the Lord appeareth to Joseph in a dream, saying, "Arise, and take the young child and his mother, and flee into Egypt, and be thou there until I bring thee word: for Herod will seek the young child to destroy him."

When he arose, he took the young child and his mother by night, and departed into Egypt: and was there until the death of Herod.

But when Herod was dead, behold, an angel of the Lord appeareth in a dream to Joseph in Egypt, saying, "Arise, and take the young child and his mother, and go into the land of Israel: for they are dead which sought the young child's life."

And he came and dwelt in a city called Nazareth.

MATTHEW 2

# *The* FINDING *in the* TEMPLE

*When Jesus was twelve, he travelled with his
parents to Jerusalem for the feast of the passover.*

And when they had fulfilled the days, as they returned, the child Jesus tarried behind in Jerusalem; and Joseph and his mother knew not of it. But they, supposing him to have been in the company, went a day's journey; and they sought him among their kinsfolk and acquaintance. And when they found him not, they turned back again to Jerusalem, seeking him.

And it came to pass, that after three days they found him in the temple, sitting in the midst of the doctors, both hearing them, and asking them questions. And all that heard him were astonished at his understanding and answers.

And Jesus increased in wisdom and stature, and in favour with God and man.

LUKE 2

# The BAPTISM of JESUS

*When Jesus was a man*
*he was baptized by his cousin,*
*John the Baptist.*

In those days came John the Baptist, preaching in the wilderness of Judaea, and saying, "Repent ye: for the kingdom of heaven is at hand."

Then went out to him Jerusalem, and all Judaea, and all the region round about Jordan, and were baptized of him in Jordan, confessing their sins.

Then cometh Jesus from Galilee to Jordan unto John, to be baptized of him. But John forbad him, saying, "I have need to be baptized of thee, and comest thou to me?" And Jesus answering said unto him, "Suffer it to be so now."

And Jesus, when he was baptized, went up straightway out of the water: and, lo, the heavens were opened unto him, and he saw the Spirit of God descending like a dove, and lighting upon him: And lo a voice from heaven, saying, "This is my beloved Son, in whom I am well pleased."

MATTHEW 3

# *The* TEMPTATION *in the* WILDERNESS

And Jesus being full of the Holy Ghost returned from Jordan, and was led by the Spirit into the wilderness.

And the devil said unto him, "If thou be the Son of God, command this stone that it be made bread." And Jesus answered him, saying, "It is written, That man shall not live by bread alone, but by every word from God."

And when the devil had ended all the temptation, he departed from him for a season. And Jesus returned in the power of the Spirit into Galilee: and there went out a fame of him through all the region round about.

LUKE 4

# The CALLING of PETER and ANDREW

*Herod heard that John was baptizing people and threw him into prison.*

Now when Jesus had heard that John was cast into prison, he departed into Galilee. From that time Jesus began to preach, and to say, "Repent: for the kingdom of heaven is at hand."

And Jesus, walking by the sea of Galilee, saw two brethren, Simon called Peter, and Andrew his brother, casting a net into the sea: for they were fishers.

And he saith unto them, "Follow me, and I will make you fishers of men."

And they straightway left their nets, and followed him.

MATTHEW 4

# The MARRIAGE at CANA

And the third day there was a marriage in Cana of Galilee; and the mother of Jesus was there. And when they wanted wine, the mother of Jesus saith unto him, "They have no wine." Jesus saith unto her, "Woman, what have I to do with thee? mine hour is not yet come." His mother saith unto the servants, "Whatsoever he saith unto you, do it."

And there were set there six waterpots of stone, containing two or three firkins apiece. Jesus saith unto them, "Fill the waterpots with water." And they filled them up to the brim.

When the ruler of the feast had tasted the water that was made wine, and knew not whence it was: (but the servants which drew the water knew;) the governor of the feast called the bridegroom, and saith unto him, "Every man at the beginning doth set forth good wine; and when men have well drunk, then that which is worse: but thou hast kept the good wine until now."

This beginning of miracles did Jesus in Cana of Galilee, and manifested forth his glory; and his disciples believed on him.

JOHN 2

A̲nd Jesus going up to Jerusalem took the twelve disciples apart in the way, and said unto them, "Behold, we go up to Jerusalem; and the Son of man shall be betrayed unto the chief priests and unto the scribes, and they shall condemn him to death."

And Jesus went into the temple of God, and cast out all them that sold and bought in the temple, and overthrew the tables of the moneychangers, and the seats of them that sold doves, and said unto them, "It is written, My house shall be called the house of prayer; but ye have made it a den of thieves."

And the blind and the lame came to him in the temple; and he healed them.

MATTHEW 20, 21

# The CLEANSING *of the* TEMPLE

# *The* LAST SUPPER

Now the first day of the feast of unleavened bread the disciples came to Jesus, saying unto him, "Where wilt thou that we prepare for thee to eat the passover?" And he said, "Go into the city to such a man and say unto him, 'The master saith, My time is at hand; I will keep the passover at thy house with my disciples.'" And the disciples did as Jesus had appointed them; and they made ready the passover.

Now when the even was come, he sat down with the twelve. And as they did eat, he said, "Verily I say unto you, that one of you shall betray me."

And they were exceeding sorrowful, and began every one of them to say unto him, "Lord, is it I?" And he answered and said, "He that dippeth his hand with me in the dish, the same shall betray me."

Then Judas, which betrayed him, answered and said, "Master, is it I?" He said unto him, "Thou hast said."

And when they had sung an hymn, they went out into the mount of Olives.

MATTHEW 26

## The AGONY in the GARDEN

And they came to a place which was named Gethsemane: and he saith to his disciples, "Sit ye here, while I shall pray." And he taketh with him Peter and James and John, and began to be sore amazed, and to be very heavy; and saith unto them, "My soul is exceeding sorrowful unto death: tarry ye here, and watch."

And he went forward a little, and fell on the ground, and prayed that, if it were possible, the hour might pass from him. And he said, "Abba, Father, all things are possible unto thee; take away this cup from me: nevertheless not what I will, but what thou wilt."

And he cometh, and findeth them sleeping, and saith unto Peter, "Simon, sleepest thou? couldest not thou watch one hour?" And again he went away, and prayed, and spake the same words. And when he returned, he found them asleep again, (for their eyes were heavy). And he cometh the third time, and saith unto them, "Sleep on now, and take your rest: it is enough, the hour is come. Rise up, let us go; lo, he that betrayeth me is at hand."

MARK 14

And they bring him unto the place Golgotha, which is, being interpreted, The place of a skull. And it was the third hour, and they crucified him. And the superscription of his accusation was written over, THE KING OF THE JEWS. And with him they crucify two thieves; the one on his right hand, and the other on his left.

And when the sixth hour was come, there was darkness over the whole land until the ninth hour. And at the ninth hour Jesus cried with a loud voice, saying, "Eloi, Eloi, lama sabachthani?" which is, being interpreted, "My God, my God, why hast thou forsaken me?"

And Jesus cried with a loud voice, and gave up the ghost.

And when the centurion, which stood over against him, saw that he so cried out, and gave up the ghost, he said, "Truly this man was the Son of God."

MARK 15

# The CRUCIFIXION

*Jesus was arrested and taken to Pontius Pilate, the governor of Judaea, who delivered him to be crucified.*

# The BURIAL *and* RESURRECTION

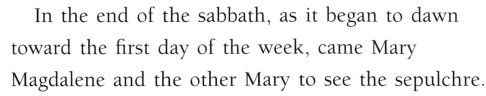

When the even was come, there came a rich man of Arimathaea, named Joseph, who also himself was Jesus' disciple: he went to Pilate, and begged the body of Jesus. Then Pilate commanded the body to be delivered.

And when Joseph had taken the body, he wrapped it in a clean linen cloth, and laid it in his own new tomb, which he had hewn out in the rock.

In the end of the sabbath, as it began to dawn toward the first day of the week, came Mary Magdalene and the other Mary to see the sepulchre.

And, behold, there was a great earthquake: for the angel of the Lord descended from heaven, and came and rolled back the stone from the door, and sat upon it. And the angel said unto the women, "Fear not ye: for I know that ye seek Jesus, which was crucified. He is not here: for he is risen, as he said."

MATTHEW 27, 28

# The ASCENSION
## *into* HEAVEN

*Forty days later Jesus
appeared before his disciples
and Mary, his mother.*

And, being assembled together with them,
[he] commanded them that they should not depart
from Jerusalem, but wait for the promise of the
Father, "which," saith he, "ye have heard of me."

And when he had spoken these things,
while they beheld, he was taken up; and a cloud
received him out of their sight.

ACTS 1

# INDEX *of* PAINTINGS

The illustrations are details of the following paintings

(ABOVE) *Front cover and page 19*
The Calling of the Apostles Peter and Andrew
**DUCCIO DI BUONINSEGNA**
*(Sienese, about 1255-1318)*
Swimming in the Sea of Galilee are many fish and an octopus, lobster, eel and ray. As fishermen, the brothers catch all kinds of creatures. Symbolically, as apostles, they will convert all kinds of humans.

(ABOVE) *Page 5 (title page)*
The Annunciation
**FILIPPO LIPPI**
*(Florentine, about 1406-1469)*
This panel's unusual shape suggests that it was meant to be installed above a doorway in a Gothic building with steep arches. The room is filled with bright sunshine – or perhaps with heavenly light, accompanying the appearance of the angel.

(ABOVE) *Page 8*
The Adoration of the Shepherds
**ADRIAEN ISENBRANT**
*(Bruges, active 1510-1551)*
Jesus is presented to us lying not in but on top of a basket crib, which makes it look almost like an altar. One shepherd plays a bladder pipe to amuse the baby. On a far-off hill, peasants dance around a bonfire, recalling the wintry Christmas season.

(BELOW) *Page 9*
The Adoration of the Magi
**BOTTICELLI**
*(Florentine, 1444/1445-1510)*
By tradition, the wise men are depicted as a young, a mature and an old man, to show all ages of humanity worshipping Jesus. The ruins of an ancient temple, now used as a stable, suggest the overthrow of pagan beliefs.

(ABOVE) *Page 4 (opposite title page)*
Madonna and Child with Saints in
the Enclosed Garden
**FOLLOWER OF ROBERT CAMPIN**
*(Netherlandish, 15th century)*
Symbols from their legends identify the holy people in the garden: Catherine, a wheel; John the Baptist, a lamb; Barbara, a tower; Anthony Abbot, a pig.

(LEFT) *Back cover and page 7 (opposite introduction)*
The Annunciation
**MASTER OF THE BARBERINI PANELS**
*(Umbrian-Florentine, active 3rd quarter 15th century)*
The dove of the Holy Ghost flies down from heaven. The vase of roses refers to Mary's purity. To give a sense of depth to the scene, the lines of the buildings and pavement meet in linear or mathematical perspective.

(ABOVE) *Page 10*
Madonna and Child and the Infant Saint John
in a Landscape
**POLIDORO LANZANI**
*(Venetian, 1515-1565)*
The Bible does not say that Jesus ever met his cousin,
John the Baptist, until they were adults at the baptism.
Artists, however, like to celebrate Jesus' humanity by
showing him as a baby with his relatives.

(BELOW) *Page 11*
The Rest on the Flight into Egypt
**GERARD DAVID**
*(Bruges, about 1460-1523)*
Mary holds grapes for Jesus to eat while, in the
background, Joseph beats chestnuts from a tree. The cool
blue and green landscape creates a quiet mood,
reassuring the viewer that the Holy Family is now safe.

(ABOVE) *Page 12*
Christ among the Doctors (obverse)
**BERNARD VAN ORLEY**
*(Brussels, about 1488-1541)*
Jesus sits under an ornate portico, but Joseph and Mary
stand in a street with brick houses typical of northern
Europe. Artists sometimes placed religious events in
familiar settings to dramatize the stories.

(ABOVE) *Page 13*
Christ among the Doctors
**MASTER OF THE CATHOLIC KINGS**
*(Castilian, active about 1485/1500)*
The gesture of putting fingers together suggests making a
point during debate. The panel comes from an altarpiece
painted for Spain's monarchs Ferdinand and Isabel. The
unknown artist is named after this work.

(RIGHT) *Page 14*
The Baptism of Christ
**JUAN DE FLANDES**
*(Hispano-Flemish, active 1496-1519)*
God the Father, wearing the triple crown of a pope,
appears in the sky with the sun and crescent moon. This
large altarpiece panel is by the same painter as the tiny
**Temptation** on page 16.

(ABOVE) *Page 15*
The Baptism of Christ
**MASTER OF THE LIFE OF SAINT JOHN THE BAPTIST**
*(Rimini, active 2nd quarter 14th century)*
The gold background symbolizes divine light. God
appears in the sky, and angels hold Jesus' robes. John the
Baptist wears camel skins, that show he was a hermit.

(ABOVE) *Page 16*
The Temptation of Christ
JUAN DE FLANDES
*(Hispano-Flemish, active 1496-1519)*
The devil, although dressed as a monk, has horns and lizard feet. Only 20 cms high, this picture was one of 47 tiny scenes depicting the lives of Jesus and Mary, painted for Spain's Queen Isabel.

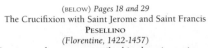

(BELOW) *Pages 18 and 29*
The Crucifixion with Saint Jerome and Saint Francis
PESELLINO
*(Florentine, 1422-1457)*
Jerome used a stone to strike his chest in penitence. Golden rays mark the Christlike wounds on Francis' hands and feet. A flaming sun and black moon recall the terrifying events that took place when Jesus died.

(ABOVE) *Pages 20 and 21*
The Marriage at Cana
MASTER OF THE CATHOLIC KINGS
*(Castilian, active about 1485/1500)*
This painting, and the one shown on page 13, formed parts of an altarpiece probably painted to mark a royal wedding in 1497. Hanging from the rafters, shields bear coats of arms of Spain and the Holy Roman Empire.

(ABOVE) *Page 22*
Christ Cleansing the Temple
EL GRECO
*(Spanish, 1541-1614)*
On the floor of the Temple at Jerusalem, a child plays with coins rather than praying. Among the animals and birds being sold as meat are a lamb, symbolic of Jesus, and white doves, referring to the Holy Ghost.

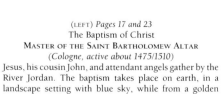

(ABOVE) *Page 25*
The Last Supper
WILLIAM BLAKE
*(British, 1757-1827)*
Jesus and his disciples and Mary Magdalen celebrate the Last Supper. In the lower right corner, Judas counts his silver even though the Bible implies he was not paid until after the betrayal.

(LEFT) *Pages 17 and 23*
The Baptism of Christ
MASTER OF THE SAINT BARTHOLOMEW ALTAR
*(Cologne, active about 1475/1510)*
Jesus, his cousin John, and attendant angels gather by the River Jordan. The baptism takes place on earth, in a landscape setting with blue sky, while from a golden heaven, God the Father and 14 saints witness the event.

(RIGHT) *Page 28*
The Crucifixion
PAOLO VENEZIANO
*(Venetian, active 1333-1358/1362)*
Mary faints into the arms of holy women, but a Roman soldier raises his hand, saluting Jesus as the Son of God. Mary Magdalen kneels beside a bloody skull, while angels collect Christ's blood in golden goblets.

(ABOVE) *Page 27*
The Agony in the Garden
**BENVENUTO DI GIOVANNI**
*(Sienese, 1436-about 1518)*
The dark grey sky shows that it is night, following the
Last Supper. Holding a sacred chalice, a glowing angel
appears to Jesus as he prays, but the apostles have fallen
asleep instead of praying with him.

(RIGHT) *Page 31*
The Lamentation
**ANDREA SOLARIO**
*(Milanese, active 1495-1524)*
Mary holds her son's body on her lap, and the apostle
John looks out at the viewers, asking us to share their
grief. On the distant hilltop, Christ's cross stands empty
between those of the two thieves.

(RIGHT) *Pages 32 and 33*
The Ascension
**JOHANN KOERBECKE**
*(German, about 1420-1491)*
Jesus rises into heaven, greeted by Old Testament figures.
Some of the apostles stare in amazement at Christ's
footprints in the rock, while John comforts Mary.

(LEFT) *Page 30*
The Crucifixion
**SANO DI PIETRO**
*(Sienese, 1406-1481)*
With stark simplicity, this picture symmetrically
arranges two holy people on either side of Jesus' cross.
His mother sits with her hands clasped in prayer, while
his friend John the Evangelist grieves.

Jesus of Nazareth © Frances Lincoln Ltd 1994
Picture index and introduction
© Frances Lincoln Ltd 1994

Extracts from the Authorized Version of the
Bible (The King James Bible), the rights in which
are vested in the Crown, are reproduced by
permission of the Crown's patentee,
Cambridge University Press.

All paintings reproduced by courtesy of the
Board of Trustees, National Gallery of Art,
Washington, including works from:
Samuel H. Kress Collection, pp 4-7, 12-15, 17-33;
Ailsa Mellon Brûce Fund, pp 8, 16;
Andrew W. Mellon Collection, pp 9-11.

First published in Great Britain in 1994 by
Frances Lincoln Limited, 4 Torriano Mews
Torriano Avenue, London NW5 2RZ

British Library Cataloguing in Publication Data
available on request

ISBN 0-7112-0871-9

Set in Berkeley Oldstyle ITC by
SX Composing, Rayleigh, Essex

Printed and bound in Italy

Designed by David Fordham

1 3 5 7 9 8 6 4 2